Foundation History

THE ROMAN EMPIRE

Fiona Reynoldson

Heinemann

Heinemann Library,
an imprint of Heinemann Educational Books Ltd,
Halley Court, Jordan Hill, Oxford OX2 8EJ

OXFORD LONDON EDINBURGH MADRID
ATHENS BOLOGNA PARIS MELBOURNE
SYDNEY AUCKLAND SINGAPORE TOKYO
IBADAN NAIROBI HARARE GABORONE
PORTSMOUTH NH (USA)

© Fiona Reynoldson 1994, 1995

The moral right of the proprietor has been asserted

First published 1994; this edition 1995

**British Library Cataloguing in Publication Data available
from the British Library on request.**

ISBN 0-431-06799-6 (Hardback)

99 98 97 96 95 10 9 8 7 6 5 4 3 2 1

Designed by Ron Kamen, Green Door Design Ltd,
Basingstoke

Illustrated by Jeff Edwards Douglas Hall Peter Hicks
Stuart Hughes Terry Thomas

Printed in China

Front cover shows Hadrian's Villa in Rome and a statue of a
Roman consul.

Acknowledgements

The author and publisher would like to thank the following
for permission to reproduce photographs:
Ancient Art & Architecture Collection: Cover, 3.3A, 4.2A
Archäologisches Landesmuseum, Schleswig: 4.1A
Archivio Moro, Rome: 4.6A
Ashmolean Museum: 1.1F
Bibliothèque Nationale: 4.3E
The Trustees of the British Museum: 1.2D, 2.1B, 2.2B, 2.4B,
2.5A, 2.9A, 2.9B, 3.12A, D and E, 4.2C, 4.4A
Simon Chapman: 4.6C
Committee for Aerial Photography, Cambridge: p25
C. M. Dixon: Front cover, 1.2E, 2.1C, 2.3A and C, 2.6E,
3.3C, 3.4B, 3.5B and C, 3.7A, C and D, 3.8A, 3.10A, 3.11A
and C, 4.1C
Sonia Halliday Photographs: 2.2C, 2.4C, 3.5A, 3.8B, 3.8D (F.
H. C. Birch), 4.5A and B
Michael Holford: Cover, 1.1A, 1.1D, 3.5B, 3.9C, 3.11D
Israel Museum, Jerusalem: 1.2C
Lion Publishing plc/David Townsend: 1.2A
Mansell Collection: p25
Alan Millard: 1.1E
Museum of London: 4.4F
The National Gallery: 4.6B
National Museum of Ireland: 4.1D
Nationalmuseet, Copenhagen: 3.2G
Dr P. J. Reynolds/Butser Ancient Farm: 3.9D
Rheinisches Landesmuseum, Trier: 3.5A, 3.10B and C
Chris Ridgers: 4.6D
Römisch-Germanisches Museum: 2.9D
Tyne & Wear Museum Service: 3.1D

Vatican Museum: 2.1A
Roger Wood: 3.8C
Woodmansterne Picture Library/Museum of London: 3.9A
We are also grateful to the following for permission to
reproduce copyright material:
Andromeda Oxford Ltd for Source 3.7B, taken from *Atlas of
the Roman World* by Tim Cornell and John Matthews, Phaidon
Press, 1982; B. T. Batsford Ltd for Source 1.2B, taken from
England Before Domesday by Martin Jones; Longman Group
UK Ltd for Source 1.3A, taken from *The Romans in Britain* by
Dorothy Morrison, 1978.

Every effort has been made to contact copyright holders of
material reproduced in this book. Any omissions will be
rectified in subsequent printings if notice is given to the
publisher.

Details of Written Sources

In some sources the wording or sentence structure has been
simplified to ensure that the source is accessible.

The Anglo-Saxon Chronicle (Trans. G. N. Garmonsway), J. M.
Dent and Sons Ltd, 1953: 4.4C
Saint Augustine, *City of God* (Ed. David Knowles), Penguin,
1972: 4.2B
D. Breeze and B. Dobson, *Hadrian's Wall*, Allen Lane, 1976:
2.6B
Julius Caesar, *Commentaries* (Ed. R. L. A. Du Pontet), Oxford
University Press, 1900: 2.7A
Simon Esmonde Cleary, *The Ending of Roman Britain*, Barnes
and Noble Books, 1989: 4.4E
Tim Cornell and John Matthews, *Atlas of the Roman World*,
Phaidon Press, 1982: 2.1D, 2.2A, 2.5B, 3.2F, 3.4C
K. Greene, *Archaeology of the Roman Economy*, Batsford, 1986:
3.4D
Catherine Hills, *Blood of the British from Ice Age to Norman
Conquest*, George Philip in association with Channel 4 TV
company, 1986: 4.3D
J. Liversidge, *Roman Britain*, Longman, 1958: 2.8A
A. Millard, *Discoveries from the Time of Jesus*, Lion, 1990: 2.3B,
2.9E, 3.11B, 3.12B and C
R. W. Moore, *The Roman Commonwealth*, English Universities
Press, 1942: 3.3D
Oxford Dictionary of Quotations, Oxford University Press, 1982:
1.1C
J. Percival, *The Roman Villa: a Historical Introduction*, Batsford,
1976: 4.1B, 4.3B and C
Michael Postan, *The Medieval Economy and Society*, Weidenfeld
and Nicolson, 1972: 4.4G
J. M. Roberts, *History of the World*, Penguin, 1980: 2.6A and C,
4.5C
R. R. Sellman, *Roman Britain*, Methuen, 1956: 2.8B
Diodorus Siculus, *Library of History* (Trans. C. H. Oldfather),
Heinemann, 1939: 2.7B
P. Salway, *Roman Britain*, Oxford University Press, 1981: 2.5E,
2.6D, 2.8C, 2.9CL.
A. Thompson, *Romans and Blacks*, Routledge, 1989: 3.2A, B, C
and E
G. I. F. Tingay and J. Badcock, *These Were the Romans*, Hulton,
1972: 3.1A
G. M. Trevelyan, *History of England*, Longman, 1926: 4.4D

CONTENTS

1.1 Words from the Past

Primary sources

Look at Source A. This is a primary source. A primary source is one that comes from the time the historian is studying. Source A is written in Latin. Latin was the main language spoken in the Roman Empire.

Questions to ask about written primary sources:

- When was it written?
- Who wrote it?
- Why did someone write it?
- Who told the writer the information for it?

You may not be able to answer all these questions about every primary source you use.

A curse written in Latin on a piece of lead. It says: 'He who stole Vilbia from me, may he waste away like water.'

Source C

Source C is different. It is a primary source. But Virgil did not write in English and he did not type his poem on this piece of paper. This is a copy.

Questions to ask about copied sources:

- If it is a copy, is it copied correctly?
- Has it been changed from one language into another?
- Has changing the language changed the sense?

Many snakes and other kinds of wild beasts live there, and the local people say that if a man crosses Hadrian's Wall he dies, unable to stand the poisoned air.

A Roman, writing about northern Britain in the 6th century AD.

I saw you picking
Dewy apples with your
    mother...
How I saw you
How I fell in love!

A poem written by Virgil in the 1st century BC.

D

SOURCE

This carving from Hadrian's Wall is from AD 142. It says: 'A detachment of the 20th Legion of Valeria and Victrix made this'.

E

SOURCE

This writing is in Greek. It says Pekysis paid his taxes on 12 July, AD 144.

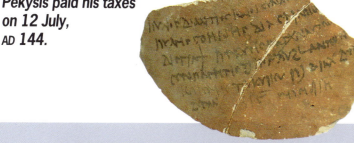

F

SOURCE

This writing is in Greek. It dates from the 1st century AD.

Procopius

Procopius (about AD 490–570) lived in the eastern part of the Roman Empire (Byzantium). He wrote books about history and geography. He also wrote about how some of the great buildings of the Roman Empire were built.

Some of his books were based on things he had seen and done. But if he had not visited a place he wanted to write about, he based his description on what other people had written about it. So we cannot rely on all he says.

Procopius fought in battles, too. He fought with the Roman army against the barbarian tribe called the Vandals, in North Africa. The Vandals had invaded the Roman Empire. The war against the Vandals ended in AD 536. But there were other barbarian tribes trying to invade the Empire.

Procopius went to fight against the Goths in Italy. This war ended in AD 540. He did not fight again.

1.2 Pieces of the Past

SOURCE

A Roman house from the 1st century AD.

Non-written primary sources

Not all primary sources are written down. Some primary sources are objects. All the sources on pages 6 and 7 are primary sources. They were made in Roman times.

Archaeologists

Archaeologists are people who dig into the ground, looking for things from the past. These things can be everyday objects like pots, mirrors, swords, shoes and combs. Archaeologists even look for whole houses. All these things are primary sources.

C

SOURCE

A sandal from about AD 74.

B

SOURCE

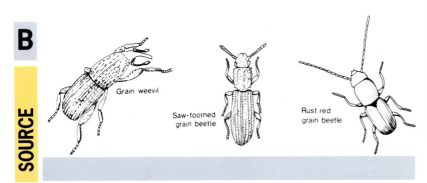

Grain weevil

Saw-toothed grain beetle

Rust red grain beetle

Drawings of insects found by archaeologists in a Roman building.

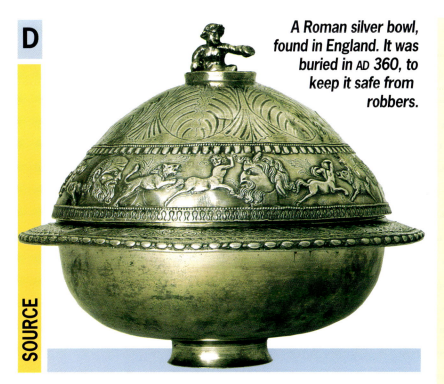

A Roman silver bowl, found in England. It was buried in AD 360, to keep it safe from robbers.

Fiorelli

Giuseppi Fiorelli (1823–96) was Professor of archaeology at Naples, Italy. He excavated the ruined city of Pompeii, which had been buried under volcanic ash in AD 79. Pompeii was found again in 1748, but the job of excavating it only began in 1860.

Fiorelli and his archaeologists cleared the ash and pumice from the streets. Fiorelli made a street plan, showing where each building was. He used plaster to preserve the shapes of the people and animals they found. The plaster shapes are in the Museum of Naples.

A picture of a woman from Italy. It dates from the 1st century AD.

1.3 Secondary Sources

Secondary sources

Secondary sources usually come from a time later than the time the historian is studying.

History books

History books, like this one on the Roman Empire, are secondary sources. People who write history books study primary sources and then write down what they have learned about the past. What they write down is a secondary source.

People who write history books do not always agree with each other. They may have used different primary sources. They may look at things differently. You must remember this when you read a history book.

B

SOURCE

Primus has made ten tiles.
That is enough.

Scratched on a Roman tile found in London.

C

SOURCE

For the last two weeks, Austalis has been wandering off on his own every day.

Scratched on a Roman tile found in London.

An artist's idea of how people in Britain lived before the Romans invaded. It has come from a history book, 'The Romans in Britain', written by Dorothy Morrison in 1978.

A

SOURCE

D

SOURCE

Sometimes people scratched things onto roof tiles.

From a history book, written in 1993.

E

SOURCE

The Romans made roof tiles in London. They were made by slaves who worked very hard. They were watched over all the time by their master.

From a history book, written in 1993.

F

SOURCE

A fashionable woman crimps her hair into rows of curls, and builds it up high.

Written by Juvenal, a Roman.

G

SOURCE

A Roman woman, drawn in 1994.

Edward Gibbon

Edward Gibbon (1737–94) was a British historian who wrote one of the most famous books ever about the Roman Empire. The book is called *The Decline and Fall of the Roman Empire.*

Gibbon was often ill as a young child, so his education kept being interrupted. So when he went to Oxford University, in 1752, he knew a lot about some things (including history) but very little about others.

Gibbon was interested in studying religion, so his father sent him to study in Switzerland. From there he travelled to France and Italy. In Italy Gibbon became interested in the Romans

and decided to write a book about them.

Gibbon's view of the Romans was affected by what he believed was right. He thought that the Roman Empire fell because the emperors were more interested in feasting, drinking and enjoying themselves than in behaving properly and doing their duty. He also tried to show that as Christianity rose the Empire fell.

Eventually Gibbon came back to live in England. He settled down to live the life of a gentleman, and to write and study. *The Decline and Fall of the Roman Empire* was published between 1776 and 1778.

2.1 Roman Rise to Power

Romulus

The city of Rome began in about 750 BC. There is a legend that it was started by a man called Romulus.

The Etruscans

The Etruscans came from Etruria, near Rome. From about 600 BC the Etruscans ruled Rome. They were good at making things from metal. They made everything from swords to mirrors of polished metal. They were good at building. They built drains and houses.

The Roman Republic from 510 BC

In about 510 BC, the Romans threw out the Etruscan king. Rome became a republic. This is a place ruled without a king or queen.

Rome gets stronger

Slowly the Romans conquered more and more land in Italy. The Romans fought off the Greeks and the Gauls (see the map on this page). By 265 BC Rome controlled Italy. About three million people lived in Italy then.

Roads, armies and Latin

The Romans built good roads. They had a strong army. They made sure the places they conquered were well ruled. More and more Italians accepted Roman rule. They spoke Latin.

SOURCE

A mirror made by an Etruscan.

Early Rome and its neighbours.

Land controlled by Greek settlers

Invasion by Gauls, 390 BC

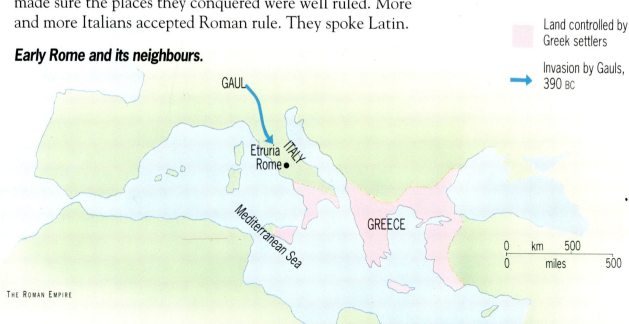

GAUL

Etruria
Rome

ITALY

Mediterranean Sea

GREECE

| 0 | km | 500 |
| 0 | miles | 500 |

B *A Roman coin made in the 1st century BC. It celebrates a Roman victory.*

SOURCE

D Have you ever seen a more richly farmed land than Italy?

SOURCE

Written by Varro, a Roman who lived in the 1st century BC.

C

SOURCE

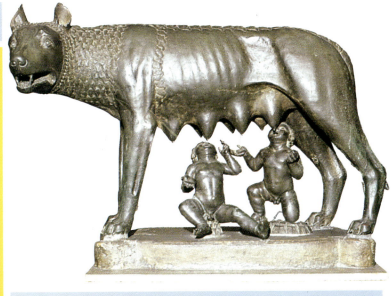

How Rome got its name.

The legend says that Romulus and Remus were the twin grandsons of a king. When he died, they were left by a river to die, to stop them ruling. They were found and raised by a she-wolf. When they grew up they decided to build a great city on the spot where they had been left to die. But they had a row. Romulus killed Remus, and named the city after himself.

Varro

Varro (116–27 BC) was a great writer who lived during the early years of the Roman Empire. He wrote books to teach the Romans about their great past. He hoped that this would make them proud to be Roman. Varro's writings had a big effect on the leaders of Rome, both during his lifetime and after.

During the civil wars in Rome Varro did not support Julius Caesar. He supported Caesar's rival, Pompey. But when Pompey was defeated, Caesar forgave Varro. Later he even made Varro his librarian.

Varro wrote over 600 books. He wrote about history, law and geography, and about education and astronomy.

2.2 Rivals for Trade

Trade

Trade is buying and selling things. The people who buy and sell things are called traders.

Roman traders

Traders can make lots of money. For instance, a Roman trader filled his ship full of jars of wine. He sailed to Sicily. He sold the wine for more than he paid for it. He made lots of money. Other traders bought and sold other things.

Traders from Carthage and Greece

However, Romans were not the only traders. There were traders in Greece and Carthage. They wanted to sell wine to people in Sicily or horses to people in Spain. Rome and Carthage started to fight over who traded where.

Hannibal

Hannibal led the Carthaginians against the Romans. He had an army of about 35,000 men and 40 elephants. He set off for Italy. Whenever he reached a big river, he floated the elephants across on rafts. In winter, in the snow and ice, Hannibal crossed the mountains into Italy.

The Romans were taken by surprise. Hannibal won battle after battle for several years. But he could never take Rome itself. In the end the Romans attacked Carthage. Hannibal fled. In 182 BC he took the poison he always carried in a ring on his finger, and died. In 146 BC, the Romans destroyed Carthage and built a new Roman city with the same name.

A The Carthaginians will not harm any Roman subjects.

The Carthaginians will not build any forts in Roman lands.

SOURCE

From a treaty between Rome and Carthage, made in 201 BC.

Hannibal

Hannibal (247–183 BC) was the son of a general from Carthage. From 228 BC to 183 BC Carthage and Rome were at war. Hannibal trained as a soldier and fought the Romans, like his father.

In 221 BC Hannibal was put in charge of the Carthage armies. In 218 BC Hannibal marched into southern Gaul. He wanted to march from there into Italy, to attack Rome. He made his army move fast. They marched 750 miles in just four months. Hannibal took elephants with him on this march, because they could carry a lot and were very strong.

Hannibal and his army (including the elephants) crossed the Alps in only fifteen days. But they were tired and running out of food, weapons and equipment.

Hannibal killed himself with poison to avoid capture by the Romans.

B

SOURCE

A Roman coin from 125 BC. It celebrates a Roman victory over Carthage in 251 BC.

C

SOURCE

The remains of the Roman city of Carthage.

Trade routes at the time of the wars with Carthage.

Trade routes between Greek cities

Trade routes between Carthaginian cities

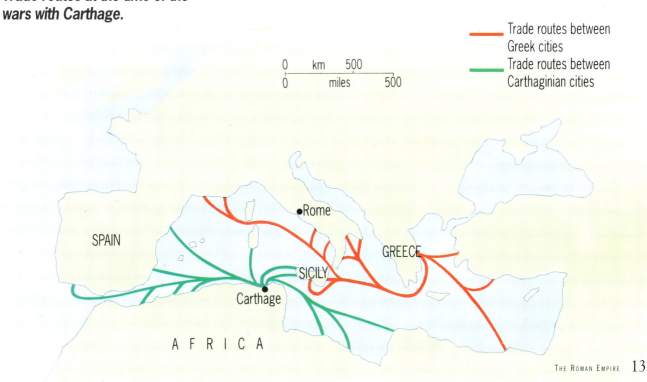

SPAIN

Rome

GREECE

SICILY

Carthage

A F R I C A

0 km 500
0 miles 500

2.3 The Roman Army

The army got bigger

The Romans had a very good army. At first it was small. But the Roman Empire grew bigger. So they needed a bigger and bigger army to conquer new lands.

Reorganizing the army

By 100 BC the Roman army was reorganized. Many men became full-time soldiers.

How the army was organized

8 men	= 1 contubernium (tent)
10 contubernia	= 1 century (80 men)
6 centuries	= 1 cohort (480 men)
10 cohorts	= 1 legion

A legion was really about 5,400 men. The 1st cohort had 600 extra men. These men worked for the whole army. Some of them were blacksmiths, cooks, messengers, clerks.

Written by Herodian. Before this time soldiers under the rank of centurion were not allowed to marry.

A **SOURCE**

Roman soldiers building a fort. This picture is of a memorial to the Emperor Trajan. It is called Trajan's column.

Soldiers also built roads and bridges.

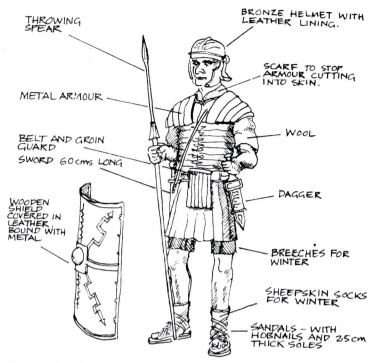

THROWING SPEAR

BRONZE HELMET WITH LEATHER LINING.

SCARF TO STOP ARMOUR CUTTING INTO SKIN.

METAL ARMOUR

WOOL

BELT AND GROIN GUARD

SWORD 60cms LONG

WOODEN SHIELD COVERED IN LEATHER BOUND WITH METAL

DAGGER

BREECHES FOR WINTER

SHEEPSKIN SOCKS FOR WINTER

SANDALS – WITH HOBNAILS AND 2.5cm THICK SOLES

A Roman Legionary.

C

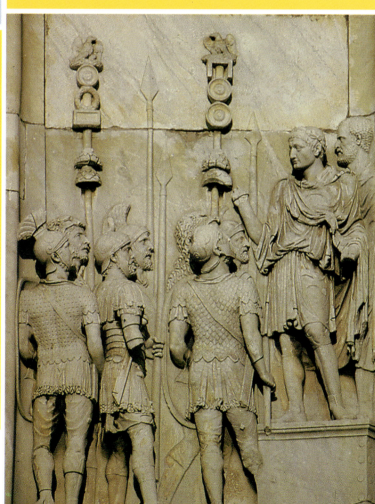

A Roman carving showing a Roman emperor talking to his soldiers.

D

They make a desert and call it 'peace'.

Written by Tacitus, a Roman, in about AD 90. He is describing how the Roman army treated the lands they conquered.

Trajan

The Emperor Trajan (AD 53–117) was a soldier, and soon became a leader of the Roman army. Trajan became emperor at a time when Rome was very unsettled. A Roman lawyer, called Nerva, adopted Trajan, who was popular in the army, as his son. Nerva then became emperor.

When Nerva died Trajan became emperor. He tried to capture more land in the east of the Empire, and his army won many battles. Trajan had a great stone column made to tell the stories of his victories. It is called Trajan's Column. (Source A).

2.4 The Roman Republic

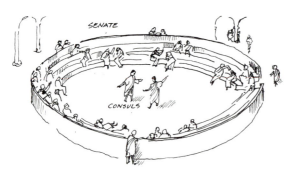

Two consuls were chosen to run the Senate and the army. If Rome was in danger they would appoint a dictator.

The Senate

The Romans made themselves into a republic in 509 BC. They did not have a king any more. Rome was run by the Senate. The men in the Senate made the laws. At first the Senate had 100 members. Later there were many more. Some of the Senators had jobs such as being judges, paying the army or governing parts of the empire.

Citizens

Roman citizens could vote for who they wanted in the Senate. Some citizens were rich. They became senators and made the laws. Sometimes the poor citizens became angry. They wanted to make laws.

Writing the laws down

In 450 BC the poor citizens insisted that Roman laws were written down. Then everyone knew what was fair.

Slowly the poor citizens won the right to have a say in making the laws. But even so the real power lay with the rich citizens.

A Roman coin made in AD 23. The letters mean 'made by permission of the Senate.'

The letters SPQR stand for 'Senate and People of Rome'. These letters were put on buildings and army standards.

Cicero

Marcus Tullius Cicero (106 BC) was a Roman lawyer and writer. He was educated in Rome and Greece. Cicero lived in Rome during its civil wars. The Senate and the army often argued. Sometimes, if things were very bad, the Senate chose a person or several people as dictator to rule Rome until they got things under control. Many people thought it would be better to have one strong leader all the time – an emperor.

But Cicero thought that Rome was better off run as a Republic. He did not support anyone who wanted total power. In 58 BC Cicero was forced to leave Rome because of his ideas. He was allowed to come back in 57 BC. In 51 BC he was even made governor of a province. But he opposed Julius Caesar when Caesar was made dictator. He also opposed Octavian, who took power after Caesar. In 43 BC he was executed for criticizing the government.

C

The ruins of the Forum in Rome. The Romans built a forum in every Roman town. It was the town centre, with an open space for meetings.

SOURCE

2.5 Building an Empire

An empire

A country has an empire when it conquers lots of other countries and takes control of them. All of the countries it controls are part of its empire.

The Roman Empire and the army

The Romans conquered more and more countries. More and more men joined the Roman army. Soon the Roman army was the biggest and best in the world. With a big army, the Romans could conquer more countries. This is how the Roman Empire grew.

The Roman Empire and trade

Many Romans made a lot of money trading all over the empire. Having an empire meant money and power for the Romans.

More lands conquered

Look at the map on the opposite page. By 30 BC all the land coloured blue had been conquered by Rome. This was a lot of land. But the Roman Empire was still growing. However, by AD 117 the Roman Empire was just about as big as it would ever be.

B SOURCE

I have given them an Empire without limits.

Said by a Roman god in a play written in the 1st century BC.

C SOURCE

The gods desire that Rome shall be the capital of all the world.

Written by Livy, a Roman playwright, in 1st century BC.

D SOURCE

Don't forget, Romans, it is your special skill to rule all peoples.

Written by Virgil, a Roman, in 1st century BC.

E SOURCE

The Romans felt that they had absolute right on their side.

From 'Roman Britain', by P. Salway, 1981.

A SOURCE

A Roman coin which shows the Greek god, Apollo.

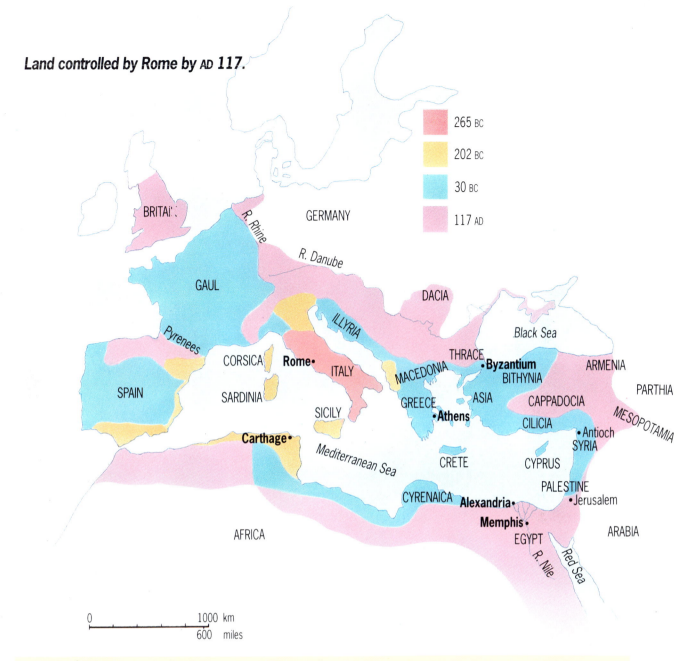

Land controlled by Rome by AD 117.

265 BC	
202 BC	
30 BC	
117 AD	

GERMANY

BRITAIN

R. Rhine

R. Danube

GAUL

DACIA

Pyrenees

ILLYRIA

Black Sea

CORSICA

Rome•

ITALY

MACEDONIA

THRACE

Byzantium

ARMENIA

SPAIN

SARDINIA

GREECE

ASIA

BITHYNIA

CAPPADOCIA

PARTHIA

MESOPOTAMIA

SICILY

•**Athens**

CILICIA

Carthage•

Mediterranean Sea

CRETE

CYPRUS

•Antioch

SYRIA

CYRENAICA

Alexandria•

PALESTINE

•Jerusalem

AFRICA

Memphis•

EGYPT

ARABIA

R. Nile

Red Sea

0 — 1000 km
600 miles

Livy

Titus Livius (59 BC–AD 17) is better known as Livy. Livy wrote *A History of Rome from its Foundation*. It was famous in his lifetime, and it still is. When he finished writing, it made up 142 books. Only books 1–10 and 21–45 have survived. The rest are lost.

Livy used earlier Roman and Greek histories to write his books. He filled in gaps with legends and stories that were commonly told about famous people and battles.

Livy spent more of his time in Padua (where he was born and grew up) than in Rome.

2.6 The Rise of the Dictators

Arguments

In the 2nd century BC, rich and poor citizens started to argue about who ran the Roman republic.

Marius and Sulla

Marius was a good general. He made the Roman army bigger and better and became very powerful in Rome. But other army leaders became powerful too. One of these was Sulla. Marius and Sulla fought until Marius died.

Pompey

The next powerful general was Pompey. He made an alliance with two other men. One was a senator called Crassus. The other was a young man called Julius Caesar.

Julius Caesar

Caesar spent ten years leading the army. He conquered the whole of Gaul. His soldiers loved him. They would follow him anywhere. Caesar decided to head back to Rome in 49 BC. He defeated Pompey and seized power for himself.

The plot against Caesar

Julius Caesar was so powerful that many of the senators were afraid of him. A group of senators got together and plotted against Caesar.

Murder – 15 March 44 BC

The senators stabbed Caesar to death in the Senate.

A SOURCE

Caesar was captured by some pirates. He was playing dice with them. He joked that he would crucify them when he was free. He did.

From 'History of the World', by J.M. Roberts, 1980.

B SOURCE

If an ordinary man could ride 50 miles a day, Caesar could ride 100 miles a day.

From 'The Great Commanders', Channel 4 TV, 1993.

C SOURCE

Caesar defeated seven legions in Spain, treated them mildly and won their obedience.

From 'History of the World', by J.M. Roberts, 1980.

D SOURCE

Caesar was a great commander because he was absolutely determined to win.

From 'The Great Commanders', Channel 4 TV, 1993.

Some of Julius Caesar's actions.

Gave land to poor citizens.

Reformed the laws.

Ruled like a king.

Built many fine buildings.

Put his friends in powerful positions.

Named a month after himself (July).

Wore purple robes, like a king.

Introduced a new calendar.

Helped many people in Spain and Gaul to become citizens.

Put up his own statue among the statues of the old kings of Rome.

Caesar

Julius Caesar (about 100–44 BC) was a soldier and a politician. He and two other powerful men (Pompey and Crassus) became leaders of Rome in 59 BC. Caesar and his army conquered Gaul (modern France). Caesar also led two expeditions to Britain, but did not conquer enough of the country to leave an army there.

In 49 BC Caesar marched to Rome. Pompey went to try to stop him. But Pompey's army was not as well trained or as loyal as Caesar's army. Pompey was beaten and fled to Egypt, where he was poisoned.

Caesar controlled the army. The Senate were scared of him. They let him give his friends important jobs, and made him dictator (ruler) for life. But they also hated him and plotted behind his back. On 15 March 44 BC a group of senators murdered him.

E

SOURCE

A bust (head and shoulders sculpture) of Julius Caesar.

2.7 Case Study 1: Caesar Invades Britain

Why did Caesar invade Britain?

Caesar was a powerful, clever general. He had won many battles in Gaul. The British had been helping the Gauls fight Caesar. This made him angry. He wanted to frighten the British. He was also curious about this wild, cold, damp land. Some people said it was full of rich jewels. Some people said the air was poisonous. Some said strange monsters lurked around the coast. Caesar did not believe all the strange stories he heard. Conquering Britain would add to his fame. So he made plans.

55 BC

It was 55 BC. Caesar set out. He had a small army. When his ships reached Britain, the British were waiting for him. Caesar's soldiers were not keen to leave the ships and wade ashore. The British looked fierce. Then the standard bearer of the Tenth Legion leapt ashore. It was a terrible thing to be a coward in the Roman army, so the others followed. They fought their way ashore and camped. A few days later a storm wrecked many of their ships. They had to repair the ships and make their way back to Gaul.

54 BC

It was 54 BC. Caesar had learnt a bit about Britain. He came back with a larger army. They landed and marched through Kent. They fought several battles. Some of the British were impressed. They decided to go over to the Roman side. In the end Caesar took some hostages. He demanded some money to be paid to Rome each year. Then he went back to Gaul.

Was invading Britain a good idea?

The Romans disagreed about whether it was worth invading Britain. Britain was a wild, faraway country. It was very difficult to get there. No one knew much about it. The sources on pages 22 and 23 give you some different views about Britain.

SOURCE A

There are many men, buildings and herds of animals. There is much wood. The money is bronze or gold.

Written by Julius Caesar, after he had been to Britain. Caesar lived from 100–44 BC.

SOURCE B

Their way of life is simple. There are many people there. Much tin is taken from Britain to Gaul.

Written by Diodorus Siculus, a Roman, in about 30 BC.

SOURCE C

Britain has gold, silver, other metals and pearls.

Written by Tacitus, a Roman, who lived from AD 56–115.

D

Caesar hurt the enemy more than he got rich. You could not take anything from people who were so poor.

SOURCE

Written by Plutarch, a Roman, who lived from AD 50–125.

E

Caesar defeated the British. He took a lot of money from them.

SOURCE

Written by Suetonius, a Roman, in about AD 120.

F

The British do not use money. They get what they want by swapping.

SOURCE

Written by Solinus, a Roman, in about AD 200.

G

Some people think that the Britons are named from the word 'brutes', because they are so cut off from the world.

SOURCE

Written by Isidorus Hispalensis, a Roman, in about AD 620.

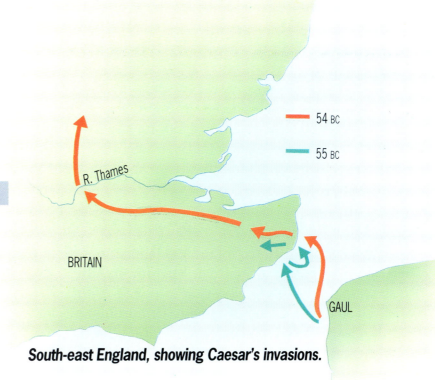

54 BC

55 BC

R. Thames

BRITAIN

GAUL

South-east England, showing Caesar's invasions.

Cassivelaunus

We do not know when Cassivelaunus was born, or when he died. By the time Julius Caesar invaded in 55 and 54 BC Cassivelaunus was the most powerful leader in the south-east of England.

Cassivelaunus' tribe, the *Catuvellauni*, had threatened nearby tribes. One of these tribes, the *Trinovantes*, asked Caesar for help. Caesar gave this as one of the reasons for taking an army to Britain. Cassivelaunus fought the Romans several times. But the Romans forced him to surrender. He gave hostages and tribute money to the Romans. No more is known of him.

The Romans called the British tribes 'savages'. They thought that the British were dirty and stupid. This is because the British did not speak Latin or Greek. They had no need to. They spoke their own language, and the languages of nearby tribes. The British did not have complicated bathing and cleaning systems like the Romans. But they had complicated trading systems, used money and made beautiful jewellery and pottery.

2.8 Case Study 2: Claudius Invades Britain

AD 43

The Emperor Claudius decided to invade Britain. He wanted to show that he was strong. But he had to have an excuse. So Claudius said that a British leader who was friendly to the Romans had been driven out of his lands. Claudius offered to help.

What happened?

The Roman army sailed to Britain and landed in Kent. There was a big battle at the River Medway and the British were thrown back. Now that it looked as if the Romans would win, Claudius came to Britain himself. He only stayed for sixteen days. But his army captured Colchester and defeated the British in the south east of Britain. Satisfied, Claudius went home to Rome.

The conquest continues

The Ninth and Fourteenth Legions marched north and west. The Second Legion continued to march along the south coast. It captured British forts one after another.

How do we know what happened?

It is not easy to find out exactly what happened. On pages 24 and 25 you will read several primary sources that do not agree with each other. You will also read some secondary sources that do not agree with each other.

B SOURCE

The Britons made a big effort to defend the River Medway. They were only driven off after a fierce, two-day battle.

From 'Roman Britain', by R. Selman, 1956.

C SOURCE

Claudius received the surrender of eleven British kings, defeated without casualties.

From a Roman carving, 1st century AD.

D SOURCE

Claudius took the triumph without any effort of his own.

Written by the Jewish historian, Josephus, in the 1st century AD.

A SOURCE

Claudius invaded our island. Some Britons welcomed the Romans, others fought them. Bit by bit the Romans conquered all of what we now call England and Wales.

From 'Roman Britain', by J. Liversedge, 1958.

E

Claudius crossed to Britain and joined the Roman army. He took over command, defeated the British and conquered Colchester.

Written by Cassio Dio, a Roman historian, who lived from AD 160–230.

F

Vespasian defeated two powerful tribes, partly under the leadership of Aulus Plautus, partly of Claudius. Claudius fought no battles.

Written by Suetonius Tranquillus, in about AD 120.

Claudius

The Emperor Claudius (10 BC–AD 54) was the nephew of the Emperor Tiberius. Claudius had a limp and a stammer.

Claudius never thought of becoming emperor. But first Tiberius and then his son Caligula went mad and were murdered. The army made Claudius emperor because there were no other men left alive in his family.

Claudius ruled from AD 41 to AD 54. He was quite successful. He led the invasion of Britain in AD 43. He also extended Roman power in North Africa. But he was careful not to start wars with the more powerful tribes on the edges of his empire. Claudius also improved the law system and wrote several history books.

Claudius married four times. Nero became the next emperor.

Maiden Castle, Dorset. A Roman force attacked the British here.

2.9 The Emperors

The Roman Republic

From 509–27 BC, Rome was a republic. There were no kings or emperors. The last years of the Roman republic were full of civil wars.

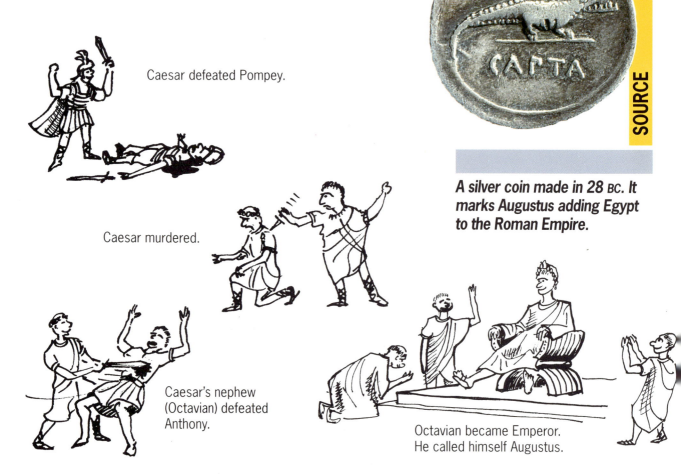

Caesar defeated Pompey.

Caesar murdered.

Caesar's nephew (Octavian) defeated Anthony.

Octavian became Emperor. He called himself Augustus.

B SOURCE

A silver coin made in 28 BC. It marks Augustus adding Egypt to the Roman Empire.

A SOURCE

A gold coin. It marks Augustus adding Armenia to the Roman Empire.

C SOURCE

The army was loyal to the emperor's family, not to the Roman Senate or people.

From 'Roman Britain', by P. Selway, 1981.

A head of the Emperor Augustus. Although it was made soon after his death in AD 14, he is made to look like a young man.

Caligula

The Emperor Caligula (AD 12–41) was not well for much of his life. We are not sure what his illness was, but something made him more and more mad. He became emperor in AD 37, after the death of Tiberius. He was cruel and often had people tortured and killed for no real reason. It was dangerous to argue with him about anything.

In AD 39 he went to Gaul with the army for a year. He may have planned to invade Britain or Germany, but did not do so. Instead Caligula made his army collect sea shells!

When Caligula returned to Rome his madness got worse. He made his horse, Incitatus, a consul (an important member of the Senate). People said he was planning to divorce his wife and marry his sister. He and his family were murdered in AD 41.

The Roman Empire

The civil wars lasted until a strong man took control. This man was Julius Caesar's nephew, Octavian. He said he was going to rule by himself. In 27 BC, he changed his name to Augustus and became the first Roman Emperor. So the years before 27 BC are called 'The Republic', and the years after are called 'The Empire'.

Augustus improved life for everyone in the Empire.

Augustus was well known for his courage and fairness. This may be because most of his enemies did not live to say otherwise.

From 'Discoveries From the Time of Jesus', by A. Millard, 1980.

3.1 Citizens

Citizens and their rights and duties

A citizen is a member of a country. A citizen has rights and duties. Citizens rights are what the laws of their country say they can do. Citizens duties are what people have to do to help their country.

Roman citizens

A Roman citizen could join the army, vote in elections and be protected by the law. A Roman citizen had to pay taxes and obey the law. There were three sorts of citizens:

Patricians They were rich. They owned farms and houses. They were often senators and made the laws.

Equites Equites were businessmen. They had less power than patricians.

Plebeians Plebeians were poor. They had very little power.

Sometimes the plebeians demanded to make the laws as well. Sometimes they went on strike or refused to fight in the army. In 450 BC the plebeians insisted the Roman laws were written down so everyone knew what they were. In 492 BC some plebeians became tribunes and were allowed to speak in the Senate.

B SOURCE

Paul and Silas were whipped and put in jail. When the soldiers found out Paul and Silas were Roman citizens, they were afraid.

From 'The Bible'.

C SOURCE

What use are laws when money calls all the tunes?

Written by Petronius in the 1st century AD.

A SOURCE

The most important split in Roman society was between the particians and the plebeians. Only patricians entered the Senate, ran the country, controlled religions. In Rome any marriage between a patrician and a plebeian was forbidden by law.

From 'These Were the Romans', by G.I.F. Tingay and J. Badcock, 1972.

Non-citizens

At first only Romans were citizens. But gradually, some free men were allowed to become Roman citizens. Women and slaves were never citizens.

Slaves

At first there were not many slaves. But as the Romans conquered more countries they took more prisoners. Many prisoners were sold as slaves. A slave had no rights. They were bought and sold like horses or pieces of furniture.

Slaves did many different jobs. Greek slaves were teachers and accountants. Other slaves worked on farms, in homes or in the mines. Some were well treated. Others were beaten or killed. The emperors Augustus and Hadrian passed laws to stop the worst treatment of slaves.

D

SOURCE

The tombstone of a woman called Regina. She was a British slave who was bought by a Roman soldier. He freed her and married her.

Paul

Paul (?–AD 64) was born in Tarsus (modern Turkey). His original name was Saul. He was a Jewish leader. He became a Roman citizen and persecuted Christians. Then he became a Christian himself. He said this was because he saw a vision of Jesus while travelling from Tarsus to Damascus. This was when he changed his name to Paul.

Paul talked about the teachings of Jesus to the people of Damascus and Jerusalem. Later he travelled all over the empire, setting up Christian groups. Paul was captured by the Romans. The Emperor Nero had him executed. Paul was later made a saint.

3.2 Barbarians

Roman views on barbarians

The Romans did not think much of anyone who lived outside the Roman Empire. They called them barbarians.

All sorts of barbarians

There were all sorts of barbarians. They were different tribes of people. The barbarians liked the look of all the things the Romans had. They liked the farms and stone built houses. They liked the towns and theatres. They liked the coins, the jewels, clothes and good food the Romans had. Often the barbarians raided the Roman Empire. The Roman army pushed them back. But when the Roman Empire got weaker the barbarians raided more and more often. In the end many barbarians settled inside the Roman Empire and some even captured Rome.

The sources on pages 30 and 31 show you some of the views the Romans had about barbarians.

A SOURCE

Too tall. Lank blonde or red hair. Light blue eyes. Upturned noses. Huge bellies. Simple minds. Quick tempers. Brave. Reckless. Drunken. Lazy. Gambling and boastful.

Various Roman descriptions of barbarians, from 'Romans and Blacks', by L.A. Thompson, 1989.

B SOURCE

Pale brown faces. Straight nose. Bright brown eyes. Brown hair. Thin lips. Not too tall.

What a Roman should look like, from 'Romans and Blacks', by L.A. Thompson, 1989.

C SOURCE

We change our hair colour to blonde because men find it more attractive.

Written about Roman women copying barbarian ways in the 1st century AD.

D SOURCE

Africans have whiter souls than the whitest of Greeks.

Written by a Roman in about AD 250.

SOURCE E

The kingdom of Ethiopia is a rich wonderland. It has much gold and a royal family descended from the gods.

Written in a Roman geography book in about AD 250.

SOURCE F

Sulpicius Galga killed thousands of Lusitanians after they surrendered. He was let off at his trial. Few people cared what happened to barbarians.

From 'Atlas of the Roman World', by T. Cornell and J. Matthews, 1982. Lusitanians came from what is now Portugal.

SOURCE G

Roman gold and silver coins from Ginderup in Denmark. They were probably buried there in 100 AD. Archaeologists think they belonged to a barbarian who was in the Roman army. He brought his money home.

G

Tacitus

Cornelius Tacitus (AD 56–120) was one of the three greatest Roman historians.

Tacitus married the daughter of the famous Roman general Agricola in AD 77. He had various jobs running the Empire.

Tacitus wrote several books. He wrote a life history of his father-in-law, Agricola. He wrote several books called *The Histories*, which tell the story of Rome between AD 14 and AD 96. These histories praise the Emperor Vespasian.

Tacitus did not just write about Romans. One of his books, *The Germania*, is about the German tribes who lived north of the Rhine and Danube rivers. He wrote that the tribes were not as keen to get money and power as Romans were. He used old sources to write this book. It was out of date even when he wrote it. He used the book to tell the Romans that they should go back to the old ways of living.

3.3 The Family

Paterfamilias and materfamilias

The father was the head of the family. He was called paterfamilias. Everyone in the house had to do as he said. His sons had to obey him even after they left home.

Women ran the house. The mother was known as materfamilias.

Women, marriage and childbirth

Women obeyed their fathers. When they married they obeyed their husbands. Parents chose who their children married. Girls could marry at 12 years of age. Most did not marry until they were 14. The night before the wedding, a girl put her toys on the household shrine for the gods. At the wedding a contract was signed and there was a party. Many women died having children. Many small children died young.

Property

In the Roman republic all of a woman's money could go to her husband's father. Later, women controlled their own belongings and had more freedom. Many Roman writers did not like this. They thought women should just run the home. Roman writers were generally men.

B SOURCE

All men rule over women. We Romans rule all men and our wives rule us!

Written by Cato, a Roman writer, who lived from 234–149 BC.

A SOURCE

Statues of a family from Palmira (in modern Syria). These people lived in the Roman Empire. But they would not have lived like a Roman family. They dressed and lived like a middle eastern family.

A Roman carving of a baby being bathed.

Boudicca

Boudicca (?–AD 62) was the wife of Prasutagus, ruler of the *Iceni* tribe in Britain. Much of Britain was under Roman rule. Prasutagus had made a deal with the Romans. He kept his kingdom in return for not fighting with them. In AD 60 Prasutagus died. He left his kingdom to the Romans and his daughters, hoping that the Romans would let his family carry on ruling. British tribes were happy to be led by women. The Romans were not. They thought that women could not rule.

The Romans took over the *Iceni* kingdom. So Boudicca led the *Iceni* against the Romans. Other tribes joined them. They burned the new Roman towns of Colchester, London and St. Albans. Many people in the towns, Roman and British, were killed. The Romans were surprised by Boudicca's success. They sent a small army which was beaten by the rebels. They then sent their main army, which had been in Wales. This Roman army beat the rebels. Boudicca killed herself rather than be caught by the Romans.

You were a faithful and obedient wife to me. You were kind and friendly. You worked hard at your spinning. You didn't show off your running of the house. You looked after my mother.

Written by a Roman about his wife in the 1st century BC.

3.4 Transport

A

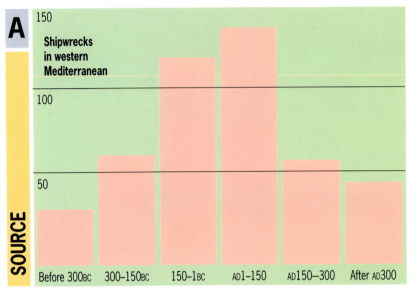

Shipwrecks in western Mediterranean

150

100

50

| Before 300BC | 300–150BC | 150–1BC | AD1–150 | AD150–300 | After AD300 |

How many ancient ships were found by underwater divers in the western Mediterranean.

C

Across the lake there is marble, food and timber. It is hard to get it by cart from the lake to the sea. It would take a lot of workmen to join the lake to the sea, but there are plenty here.

From a letter written by Pliny to the Emperor Trajan in about AD 112.

Types of transport

The two main types of transport were by road or ship. Transport was very important to the Romans.

A painting of a Roman ship.

B

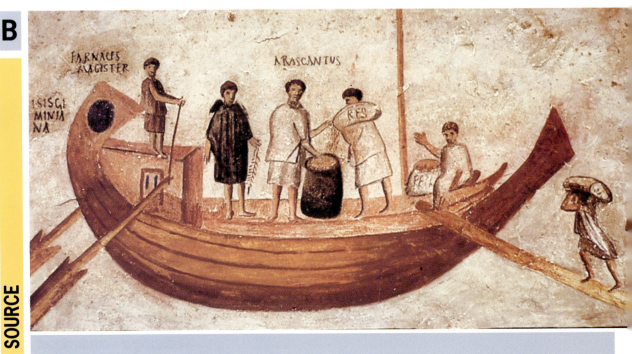

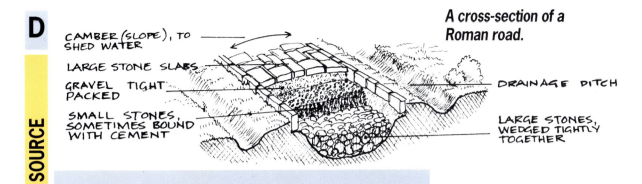

CAMBER (SLOPE), TO SHED WATER

LARGE STONE SLABS

GRAVEL TIGHT PACKED

SMALL STONES, SOMETIMES BOUND WITH CEMENT

DRAINAGE DITCH

LARGE STONES, WEDGED TIGHTLY TOGETHER

A cross-section of a Roman road.

The importance of transport

Rome had a huge empire. There were three reasons why the Romans needed good roads and lots of ships.
1 The Roman army needed to move about quickly.
2 Carts and ships had to carry food all over the empire.
3 The Romans had to collect taxes (in coins) and carry them back to Rome or to other cities.

How do we know – roads

There are still thousands of miles of Roman roads. We can look at the old Roman roads to see how they were made.

The Romans wrote books about their roads. One of these, the 'Antonine Itinerary', lists 225 routes all over the Roman Empire. It also says how far it is between towns. Roman writings show that people travelled easily from place to place. St. Paul's travels in 'The Bible', could only have happened with good road and sea transport.

How do we know – ships

There are many paintings and mosaics (see Source B) that show ships. Roman books and letters tell us about the grain and wine that was carried in ships from places like North Africa to Italy. Underwater divers have found old Roman ships that have sunk, and these tell us a lot about how the ships were made and what they carried.

The Romans built canals as well and we can still see parts of these in places like Germany and Britain.

Plutarch

Plutarch wrote books on politics, philosophy and religious beliefs. He wrote about the lives of several emperors. He also wrote about other famous people from time to time, for example Cicero.

Plutarch's books are full of details about how the Romans lived. He also described the way that they did various things, including building roads built by the army:

They were built straight across the countryside. They were paved with cut stones and supported underneath with lots of tightly-packed gravel. Hollow ground was filled in. Deep ravines that cut across the route had bridges built across them.

3.5 Trade in the Empire

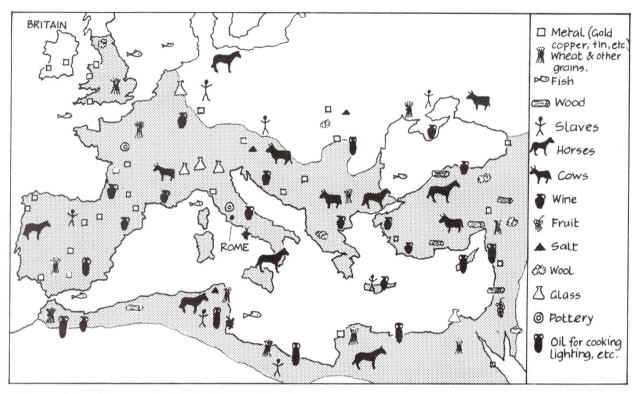

Legend:
- Metal (Gold copper, tin, etc.)
- Wheat & other grains.
- Fish
- Wood
- Slaves
- Horses
- Cows
- Wine
- Fruit
- Salt
- Wool
- Glass
- Pottery
- Oil for cooking lighting, etc.

BRITAIN
ROME

Some of the things traded in the Roman Empire.

A Roman carving of a ship carrying wine barrels.

A

SOURCE

B

SOURCE

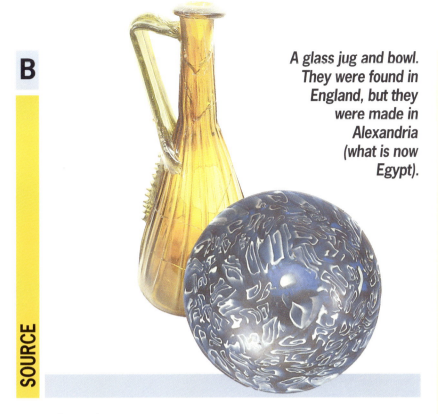

A glass jug and bowl. They were found in England, but they were made in Alexandria (what is now Egypt).

Barry Cunliffe

Barry Cunliffe is a 20th century archaeologist. He excavated many important Roman sites in Britain.

Hengistbury

In 1979 Cunliffe began to excavate Hengistbury Head. This is a headland that faces into the English Channel opposite the Isle of Wight. There was an important port here from about 100 BC.

The archaeologists found evidence that Roman traders had brought food and other goods into Britain. These included figs, Italian wine, Armorican (modern France) pottery and expensive glass. The merchants traded these goods for things produced in Britain that Rome needed.

Local trade

Trade took place throughout the Empire. But some goods were also traded locally. For example, a farmer in Italy grew olives and picked them. He put them on a cart and drove them to the nearby town to sell them. With the money that he made he could buy something that he needed. Maybe he bought some meat at the butcher's shop.

C

SOURCE

Storage jars for grain. They were buried to keep the grain cool. These jars were found in Ostia, the port that was closest to Rome.

3.6 Roman Towns and Cities

The Romans built many cities and towns all over the empire. If people in Britain wanted to build a town, they could send to Rome for a town plan like the one below.

Roman towns often needed walls to defend them.

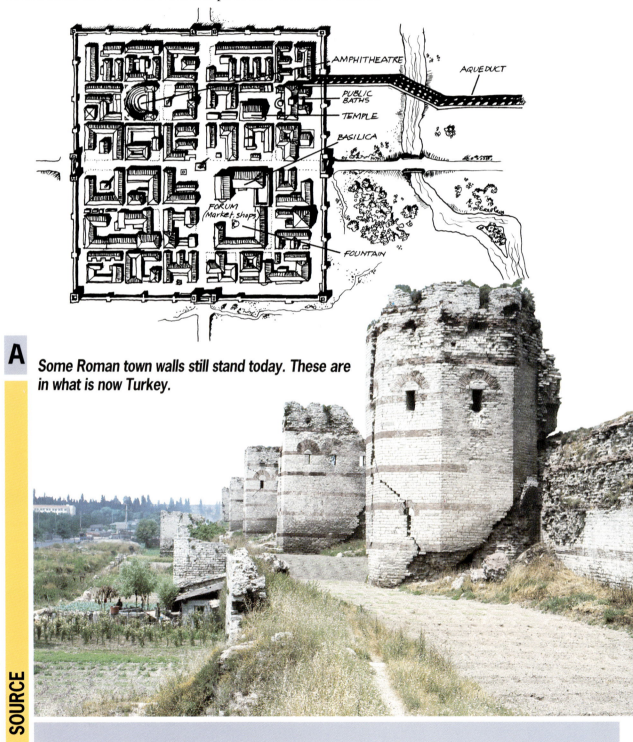

AMPHITHEATRE

AQUEDUCT

PUBLIC BATHS

TEMPLE

BASILICA

FORUM (Market, shops)

FOUNTAIN

A *Some Roman town walls still stand today. These are in what is now Turkey.*

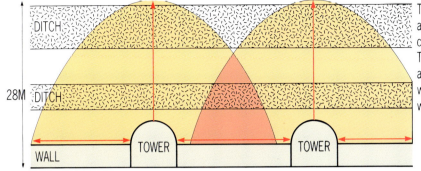

DITCH

28M

DITCH

WALL | TOWER | TOWER

Town defences after the 4th century AD. Towers were added to the walls. Ditches were redug.

Area reached by weapons fired from the walls.

Area in front of walls, out of reach of defenders weapons.

Direction and distance weapons could be fired from town walls.

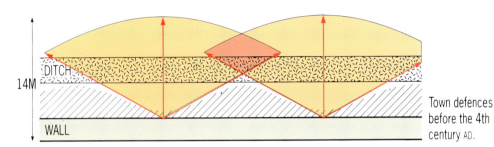

DITCH

14M

WALL

Town defences before the 4th century AD.

Towns and money

Lots of people lived in towns. They all earned money. They all needed food. So farmers brought chickens, eggs, pigs and so on to the towns to sell. The people who lived in the towns paid for the food in Roman coins. So more and more Roman coins were used and moved around the empire.

A gold coin. People all paid taxes in Roman coins. Taxes were used in lots of ways. They were used to build everything from sewers to theatres. They were used to pay the army.

SOURCE

Constantine

Constantine (?–AD 337) was made joint emperor of Rome in AD 306. In AD 312 he fought and beat Maxentius, the other emperor, and ruled alone. In AD 313 Constantine passed a law that made Christianity an acceptable religion and became a Christian.

In AD 326 Constantine started to build the city of Constantinople (now Istanbul) on the site of an old town called Byzantium. The city was finished in AD 330. It copied many of the buildings of Rome.

3.7 Buildings in Towns and Cities

SOURCE

A Roman carving of a shop.

Roman buildings

The Romans built houses, theatres, shops and temples. Many buildings were made from stone or brick. The stones or bricks were stuck together with concrete.

Roman concrete

The Romans invented concrete. They mixed cement, water, sand and bits of stone together. It made the buildings very strong.

This building was used for public games and races. The arches of the building carry all the weight, and because the building is in a circle all the arches support each other.

B

SOURCE

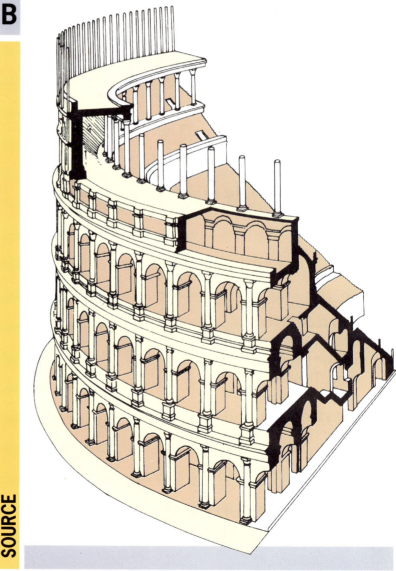

C

SOURCE

The public baths in Bath, England. The Victorians rebuilt the baths. It shows what they thought Roman baths were like.

Rich and poor

Rich people used marble to make their grand buildings beautiful. Poorer people made houses with wood and thatch or tiles.

D

SOURCE

A Roman carving of a shop.

Vespasian

Emperor Vespasian (?– AD 79) was a successful leader in the Roman army. In AD 43 he was in charge of a legion in the invasion of Britain. He became more and more powerful.

In AD 69 the Emperor Otho died. The army that was fighting with Vespasian in the Middle East made him emperor. Vespasian went to live in Rome.

Vespasian organized a lot of building in Rome. He started building the Colosseum, a huge arena, which would be able to hold 50,000 people. Work began on the Colosseum in AD 70. When Vespasian died it was still not finished. It was finished by his sons by AD 82.

3.8 Living in Towns and Cities

Public toilets in a Roman town in Africa. The Romans often built toilets like these directly over stone sewers, which carried the waste away at once. There were no sewers in the parts of the cities where the poor lived. These places were not as clean. This meant that more people became ill.

Rome in AD 1

By AD 1 there were over 1 million people living in Rome. This was a huge number for those days.

Rich and poor

Rich people lived in town houses. A town house was called a domus. The rooms were built around a courtyard. Poor people lived in blocks of flats. These were called insulae. They were badly built. They often burnt down.

An aqueduct in Africa. It took water 60 miles to the Roman city of Carthage. It took 21 years to build.

C

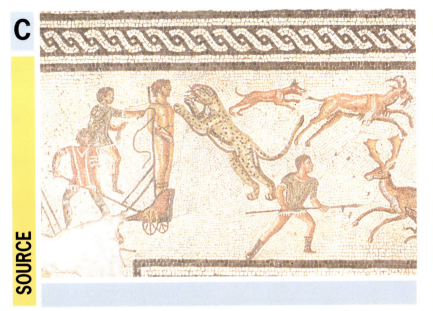

A Roman mosaic from Africa. It shows gladiators fighting animals, and a prisoner being fed to a leopard.

Fire brigade

Emperor Augustus set up a fire service. There were 7,000 men in it. The firemen used handheld pumps.

Entertainment

Emperors put on big shows to keep the people happy. There were gladiator fights, chariot races and plays.

Spartacus

Spartacus was a gladiator. In 73 BC he led a rising of the slaves in southern Italy. They beat two Roman armies. More people joined them with each success. Spartacus' army probably had about 90,000 men at its biggest.

The rebels worked their way up Italy towards Rome. By 71 BC Spartacus and his men were tired of war. They decided to go back to southern Italy and settle down. But they were attacked by another Roman army. They were beaten. Spartacus was killed in battle.

D

A Roman theatre in Ephesus (in what is now Turkey).

3.9 Life in the Countryside

Farms

Most people in the Roman Empire lived in the countryside. They grew food and kept animals.

Rich Romans

Some Romans were very rich. They owned huge farms. Sometimes they owned farms in different places. A rich woman called Melania owned farms in Italy, Sicily, Africa, Spain and Britain. This was in the 4th century AD. She employed people to run her farms. They paid her rent.

All over the empire

The Roman Empire was enormous. In Britain it was cold and wet. Farmers kept cows and sheep and grew crops like oats and wheat. In North Africa it was hot. Farmers kept goats and grew crops like dates, grapes, figs and wheat.

The plan of a Roman farmhouse did not change much over the years.

A modern archaeologist said this about farmhouses in the Middle East under all the years of Roman rule.

A modern reconstruction of a dining room in a rich Roman's farmhouse in about AD 350.

How they lived

Archaeologists have dug up many Roman country houses called villas. These were the homes of better-off farmers. Poorer people had wooden, thatched houses. These have not survived.

Farmers grew enough food to feed their families. If they had any spare food they sold it. A farmer who sold food could pay his taxes and buy pottery, brooches and tools. If archaeologists find things like this around farms, they know that a farmer was trading his food for other things.

C SOURCE

A Roman mosaic. It shows a house in North Africa.

D SOURCE

Columella

Columella was born in the early part of the first century AD. He was born in Spain. He joined the Roman army as a young man. Columella was not just a soldier. He also owned land in central Italy. He was more interested in farming than in fighting. He spent more and more time away from the army, managing his lands.

Columella had lots of ideas about how the old ways of farming could be improved.

Between AD 60 and AD 65, Columella wrote twelve books about farming, called *The Countryside*. He gave advice about how to make sure that the workers worked hard and how to make sure that the right crops were grown on the right soil. Many Roman landowners read his books and acted on his advice. He died in about AD 70.

Many poorer farmers would have lived in houses like this in Roman Britain.

3.10 Roman Villas

What was a villa?

'Villa' is a Latin word. It means a house in the country or a farm. Most people think of a villa as a large Roman country house with a farm. Villas were fairly simple at first. Later, they were rebuilt in a more grand style. The farmworkers or slaves lived in one part of the villa. The owners lived in another part.

Everywhere the Romans went people copied their villas. There are Roman style villas from Britain to North Africa.

A Roman painting from about AD 150. It shows a farm in what is now Germany.

A

SOURCE

Hypocausts

The richest people had baths and underfloor heating. This underfloor heating was called a hypocaust. There were beautiful wall paintings and mosaics on the floor.

THE DINING ROOM AND HYPOCAUST

A Roman statue of a ploughman. It comes from what is now Germany.

A Roman mosaic from about AD 320. It shows a villa in North Africa.

Cogidubnus

Cogidubnus ruled land on the south coast of Britain from about AD 43. The centre of his kingdom was Chichester. He seems to have accepted the Roman way of life. The Romans gave him more power in return for his help.

Cogidubnus was probably made a senator by Emperor Claudius in AD 47 as another reward.

3.11 Religious Beliefs

Spirits

The Romans believed spirits protected their homes. One of these was Vesta. She was goddess of the hearth. Another one was Janus. He was god of the doorway.

Roman goddesses and gods

The Romans also worshipped many gods. Some of them are listed below:

Jupiter	chief god.
Juno	goddess of women and Jupiter's wife.
Venus	goddess of love.
Neptune	god of the sea.
Mars	god of war.
Minerva	goddess of wisdom and war.
Diana	goddess of hunting.
Apollo	god of the sun.
Ceres	goddess of harvest.

An order given by the emperor in the 1st century AD.

A temple of the Roman god Jupiter. This temple is in North Africa.

C

SOURCE

A temple of the Persian god, Mithras. It was built underground in Rome.

Romans and other peoples' gods

The Romans were very easy-going about other peoples' gods. Often they just adopted new gods or goddesses wherever they went.

Christianity

This easy-going attitude seems to have changed when the Romans came in contact with Christianity. This was partly because they had to give up all the other gods to become Christian.

D *Sul was the local god in Bath, England. This is probably a carving of Sul, changed so that he also looks like the Roman goddess Minerva.*

SOURCE

Apollonius

Apollonius was a teacher and philosopher in the first century AD. He travelled all over the Roman Empire. He was interested in all the religions in the Empire and the world. He wrote about his beliefs, but few of his writings have survived. It is hard to work out what he believed.

The Roman emperors did not like him teaching his beliefs. They threatened to execute him. We do not know how he died.

3.12 The First Christians

Jesus Christ

Jesus Christ was a great teacher. He taught about living a good life, about believing in God and about life after death. Jesus was executed by the Romans in about AD 33. By this time there were many people who followed his teachings. They thought he was the son of their God. Jesus' followers were called Christians.

Christians and the Roman Empire

Christians said they could not worship all the Roman gods. They believed that they could only worship the Christian God. They believed worshipping lots of gods was wrong. This made some of the Roman emperors and people angry. Many Christians were killed.

B SOURCE

The Christians were torn apart by dogs and killed. Some were fixed to crosses, or burned to light up the night.

Written by Tacitus, a Roman, who lived from AD 56–115.

C SOURCE

The Christians swear not to steal, rob or commit adultery.

Written by Pliny, a Roman, who lived from AD 24–79.

A SOURCE

A British painting of Christians praying. It was painted in the 4th century AD.

D

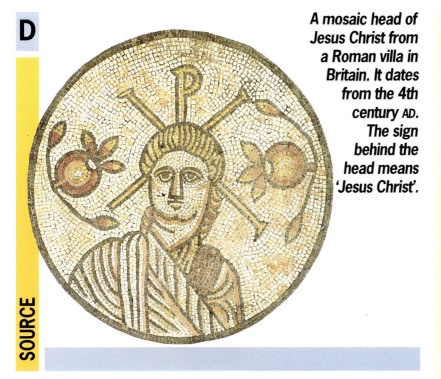

A mosaic head of Jesus Christ from a Roman villa in Britain. It dates from the 4th century AD. The sign behind the head means 'Jesus Christ'.

Theodosius I

Theodosius (AD 346–395) was a soldier who fought barbarians called the Goths in AD 378. He became emperor of the Eastern Roman Empire in AD 379. He had to fight off other barbarian tribes after he became emperor, including the Visigoths.

Theodosius was also known as Theodosius the Great. He was a Christian and tried to spread Christianity in his Empire. He did not let people follow any religion. He stopped people worshipping in ways that he thought were against the ideas of Christianity.

The Roman emperor becomes a Christian

Gradually some Romans wanted to become Christians. The Emperor Constantine became a Christian in AD 324. After this more and more important people became Christians. Soon Christianity was the official religion of the Roman Empire.

E

Pieces of silver from Britain. They date from the 4th century AD.

4.1 The Empire in Crisis

The Roman Empire by AD 100

At first it seemed the Romans would conquer the world. They took Greece, Spain, Gaul and many other lands. By AD 100 the Roman empire was huge (see map on page 19).

AD 117 – the empire stops growing

Hadrian became emperor in AD 117. He saw the empire had grown as much as it could. Barbarians were all around the edges of the empire. To conquer more land would need a bigger army. This would cost a lot of money. Hadrian felt enough was enough. He built a wall in Britain, to keep out the northern tribes. It was called Hadrian's Wall. The Romans built forts and walls all around the empire.

Problems in the empire

The population in the Roman Empire fell. So there were fewer people to pay taxes, or join the army. We are not sure why the population fell. Maybe changes in the weather meant bad harvests and too little food. Maybe raids by tribes meant that farmers gave up growing food in some places. Maybe new diseases killed off many people.

Falling trade – 3rd century AD

In the 3rd century AD, tribes began to break through the forts and walls to raid the empire. It was dangerous to travel by road or ship. Traders did not want to travel. British people could not buy glass from Egypt.

B SOURCE

5,000 a day are said to have died from the plague in Rome, and more in the country. It is possible that the plagues were smallpox and measles.

From 'Plagues and People', by W. McNeill, 1976. He was writing about illness AD 251–66.

A boat from Denmark. Danish pirates raided the Roman Empire in the 4th century AD. They may have used boats like this.

A SOURCE

C SOURCE

A Roman fort, built in Britain in AD 275. It was one of many built to protect Britain against pirates.

Towns

There was less and less trade. So towns got smaller. Shops were left empty. Buildings fell down.

The Romans leave Dacia – AD 270

The barbarians in the east raided Dacia (see map on page 19) again and again. It was AD 270. The Roman army packed up and left Dacia. This was the beginning of the end of the Roman Empire.

D SOURCE

Hadrian

Hadrian (AD 76–138) worked for the Emperor Trajan. Trajan was so pleased with him he even adopted him as his son.

In AD 117 Trajan died. Hadrian was made emperor. He travelled around the edges of the Empire to check how well they were defended. He wanted to keep the Empire strong.

Between AD 120 and AD 121 he was in France and Britain. In Britain he saw that the border with the northern tribes in Scotland was badly defended. He had a wall built which ran from one side of the country to the other. The wall had forts scattered along it. It is the famous Hadrian's Wall, which still divides England from Scotland.

While he was emperor the Empire did not lose any land to invaders.

Pieces of Roman silver, found in Ireland. The Romans never conquered Ireland. They probably paid a pirate leader not to raid them.

4.2 The Collapse of the Empire

The army

By the 3rd century AD there were not enough soldiers to defend the Roman Empire. Soldiers were rushed to wherever there was trouble. Also emperors forced men to join the Roman army because there were not enough volunteers.

The edges of the empire

There were lots of barbarian tribes around the edges of the Roman Empire. Some emperors allowed these tribes to move into the empire as long as the men agreed to fight in the Roman army.

Splitting the empire – AD 285

The emperor decided he could not run the whole empire any longer. So he split it into two parts. There was an eastern empire and a western empire. This still didn't help matters. The population fell more and more. The people who were left had to pay more and more taxes. But still the tribes outside the empire attacked and attacked.

The fall of Rome – AD 410

The attacks got worse and worse. In AD 410, tribes of Goths attacked Rome. In AD 476, the last Roman emperor was overthrown. The western Roman Empire had collapsed. Only the eastern empire was left.

A SOURCE

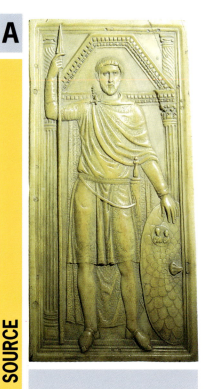

The Roman general Stilicho. He was a Vandal who fought for Rome.

B Should the Romans have trusted the defence of Rome to the gods?

SOURCE

Written by a Christian, who lived from AD 354–430.

C

SOURCE

This mosaic shows of a Vandal who has captured a Roman villa in North Africa. It dates from AD 490.

Stilicho

Stilicho (?–AD 408) was born into a barbarian tribe – the Vandals. He was a soldier who hired himself out to whoever would pay him. He fought for the Romans and then became an officer in the Western Roman Empire. He was rewarded with jobs, and became more and more powerful.

But Stilicho began to take power for himself, without waiting to be given it. From AD 395 until AD 408 he ran the Western Roman Empire. He was not called 'emperor', but he had all the real power. He was executed in AD 408, by Emperor Honorius.

The barbarian invaders of the Roman Empire in the 5th century AD.

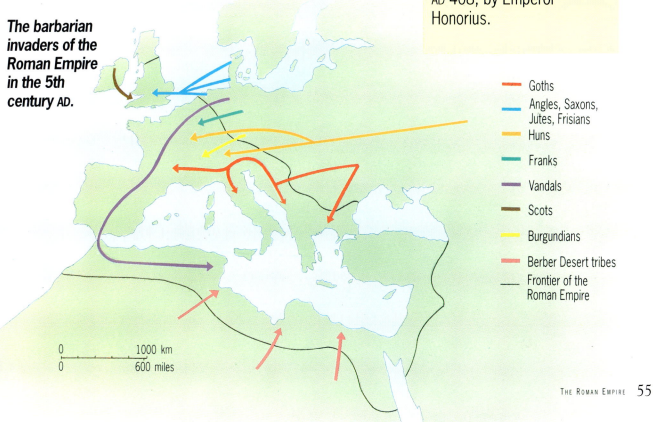

— Goths
— Angles, Saxons, Jutes, Frisians
— Huns
— Franks
— Vandals
— Scots
— Burgundians
— Berber Desert tribes
— Frontier of the Roman Empire

0 1000 km
0 600 miles

4.3 The Collapse of the Empire: Gaul

Roman Gaul

Gaul was made up of what is now France, Belgium and parts of Germany.

The invasion of Gaul.

The Franks

The Franks wanted to live like the Romans. Modern historians think that the Franks did not kill all the Romans in Gaul, or destroy all the farms. They wanted the farms themselves. Some Franks fought for the Romans against the Vandals. But gradually the Franks took over Gaul.

A Death, sorrow, destruction, fire.

SOURCE

From a poem about barbarians destroying Gaul. It was written in the 5th century AD.

B Roman villas still existed. They became the centres of villages.

SOURCE

From 'The Roman Villa', by J. Percival, 1976.

C Leontius (a Roman who lived in Gaul) owns three villas.

SOURCE

Written in about AD 550.

D Before the 5th century all the things that were buried with the dead were Roman things. During the 6th century Frankish things were buried in the graves.

SOURCE

From 'Blood of the British', by C. Hills, 1986.

Pieces of a sword found in the grave of a Frankish leader. The grave dates from about AD 482. The sword is decorated in a Roman style.

Clovis

Clovis (AD 466–496) became king of the Salian Franks (a barbarian tribe) in AD 481.

Clovis beat the Roman leader Syagrius, who was ruling in Gaul (modern France). His kingdom now covered what is now northern France and Belgium.

Clovis married in AD 493. His wife was a Christian princess, called Clotilda. Her father ruled Burgundy (in southern France). Clovis became a Christian in AD 496.

Clovis added more and more land to his kingdom, but the centre was always in the area around modern Paris.

Coins and taxes – AD 410

The Romans lost Gaul. Then they lost Britain. The Roman army left. After AD 410, there were no more Romans to collect taxes. The Romans stopped sending coins to Britain too.

The end of trade

Ordinary people had no money to buy tools, pots, plates, knives and glasses. Farmers went back to just growing enough food for themselves and their families. They did not need to grow more food to sell so that they could pay their taxes. This was the end of the Roman system of buying and selling with money.

The end of the towns

Without taxes and trade there was no reason to have towns. People moved from the towns to the country, to grow food. No one lived in towns so the shops, houses and theatres fell down.

A **SOURCE**

A Roman belt buckle. This one was worn by an Englishman buried in Essex in AD 400.

B **SOURCE**

Towns were destroyed. Survivors were killed or made into slaves forever.

A description of the Angles invading in AD 530, by a British monk who hated the English.

C **SOURCE**

1 Cerdic and Cynric took the Isle of Wight and killed a few men.

2 Cerdic and Cynric took the Isle of Wight and killed many men.

Two versions of the victory of two English chiefs. An English monk re-wrote the book.

D **SOURCE**

We can imagine the Anglo-Saxon men storming camps, burning towns, and driving away the Roman Britons.

From 'History of England', by G.M. Trevelyan, 1926.

Angles and Saxons

When the Romans left, the Angles and Saxons moved in. They came from places like modern day Germany and Denmark. They settled in the part of Britain now called England (which means land of the Angles).

E

SOURCE

The number of Anglo-Saxons who came to Britain was probably around tens of thousands. There were millions of Roman Britons.

From 'The Ending of Roman Britain', by A.E. Cleary, 1989.

G

SOURCE

We cannot take it for granted that the Anglo-Saxons killed all the Roman Britons.

From 'Medieval Society and Economy', by M. Postan, 1978.

F

SOURCE

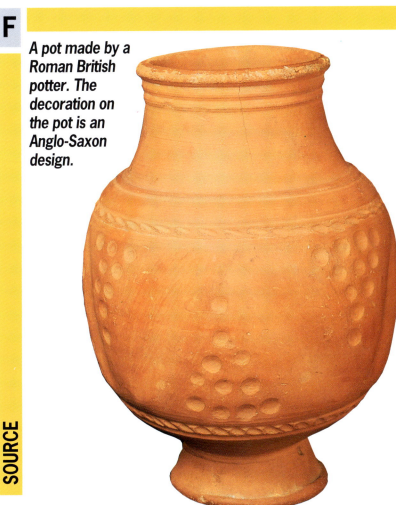

A pot made by a Roman British potter. The decoration on the pot is an Anglo-Saxon design.

Gildas

Gildas (about AD 500–572). wrote a book called *On the Ruin of Britain*. It was about the Saxon invasions of Britain. We think that Gildas was a monk, probably living in a monastery near what is now Glastonbury in Somerset.

Gildas' history is one of the very few pieces of written evidence to survive from the time of the Saxon invasions. He describes a battle at a place called Badon Hill where a British leader, called Aurelianus, defeated the Saxons. Some people think Aurelianus could be the King Arthur of the legends. But we do not know how accurate Gildas' information is.

Constantinople – capital of the eastern empire

It was AD 330. The Emperor Constantine built a new capital in Turkey. He named it after himself. The city of Constantinople became very famous. It is now Istanbul, in Turkey.

A mosaic showing Justinian's wife, Theodora, giving a gift to the Italian church.

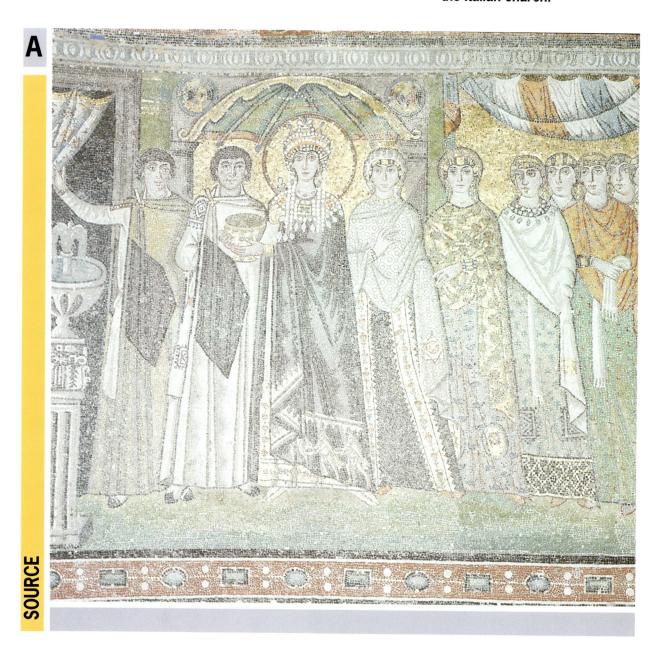

A

SOURCE

Justinian and the eastern empire

The eastern empire was quite strong. In AD 554, the Emperor Justinian recaptured Rome. But not for long. The Roman Empire in the west had gone for good. But the eastern empire went on. There were Roman buildings in Constantinople and Roman laws were obeyed. This lasted for nearly a thousand more years.

The Church of St. Sophia, in Constantinople. Justinian had it built.

Justinian

Justinian (AD 482–565) was made emperor of the Eastern Roman Empire in AD 527. He wanted to win back the parts of the Roman Empire which had been lost by earlier emperors.

In AD 533, Justinian took his army into Africa. He won back all the land there that had been lost to the barbarian Vandal tribe. From there he moved into Italy. He fought the Ostrogoths. The fighting lasted from AD 535 to AD 540. Justinian won. He then moved into Spain in AD 551. This time his army beat the Visigoths.

4.6 The Importance of Rome

Spreading ideas

The Roman Empire was huge. The Romans made it safe for people to travel, so they did. They talked about new ideas, like Christianity. The ideas spread all over Europe. Roman things spread all over Europe too. Men sailed ships all around the coasts of the Roman Empire. It was possible to buy wine and grapes in places like Britain where it was too cold to grow them.

Today

There are still many signs of the Roman Empire today.

- The Latin language is used for many things, like the names of plants.

A

SOURCE

Italian fascists in the 1920s. Some are dressed like Romans. They wanted Italy to have a great empire again, like Rome.

B

SOURCE

A picture of a Roman scene, painted 1,300 years after Rome fell.

- Many of our words come from the Latin: video, navy, public, legal.
- There are many ruins of Roman buildings and roads all over Europe.
- Many of our roads today run along the same routes as Roman roads.
- Many laws in Europe are based on Roman laws.

D *A British coin. The letters 'D.G. Reg' are short for the Latin for 'By God's Grace: Queen'.*

C *A building in Oxford, England. It is built in the Roman style, but was not built until the 1700s.*

Mussolini

Benito Mussolini (1883–1945) started the Fascist Party in Italy.

In 1922 Mussolini took power in Italy. He wanted to try to make Italy as great as it had been under the Romans. He was keen on things being organized.

In 1936 Mussolini took over Abyssinia (modern Ethiopia). In 1939 he moved into Albania. He was an ally of Hitler, the leader of the Nazi Party in Germany. Italy joined the Second World War on the side of Germany in 1940. The Italians rebelled against Mussolini in 1943. The Germans saved him, but he was captured and shot in 1945.